Nicholas & Payson—
Thanks!
Enjoy The Year—

Dave
7-2021

COVID
THROUGH
THE LENS

COVID THROUGH THE LENS

2020 Photography Yearbook

David J. Bell

gatekeeper press
Columbus, Ohio

Covid Through the Lens: 2020 Photography Yearbook

Published by Gatekeeper Press
2167 Stringtown Rd, Suite 109
Columbus, OH 43123-2989
www.GatekeeperPress.com

The editorial work for this book is entirely the product of the author. Gatekeeper Press did not participate in and is not responsible for any aspect of this element.

ISBN (hardcover): 9781662910302

Printed in the U.S.A.

FOREWORD AND INTRODUCTION

Welcome!

Thank-you for purchasing my journey through the year 2020 or "Covid Through The Lens". This was a year which will be remembered for decades, if not centuries!

My goal with this book, as an active and ambitious photographer, is to provide a chronological log to the year—January to December and that is how the book is organized.

As you page through the book, watch for the changing seasons, the evolving beauty of winter to spring, finally, summer then fall, and a return to winter! My home base is a photographer's paradise—mountains, deserts, mesas, rivers and streams, aspen forests, ranches, expansive vistas, and wildlife galore!

I am a resident of Pinedale, and have raised my family in this wonderful community tucked into the foothills of the Wind River Mountains of western Wyoming. I can be found most anytime on the hiking trails of western Wyoming or on a photography safari across Wyoming and surrounding states.

I'd like to thank my wonderful wife for her generous support of this hobby. We enjoy our time together in the field exploring the beauty of our country.

2020 was quite a year, but for those of us in rural parts of the country, the dreaded impacts of the COVID virus were greatly minimized. In fact, as I review my life versus those of my friends in other parts of the country, life was mostly normal—except the news every day.

We took advantage of the year to shoot over 100,000 images. Every image in this book was taken during 2020.

I hope you enjoy the book and the beauty of nature.

–Dave Bell, Pinedale
Email: davidj_bell@msn.com
Web: www.wyomingmountainphotography.com
Facebook: Wyoming Mountain Photography

CONTENTS

JANUARY

Normal Year

January began a new year and by all signs it was going to be another awesome year for America. It was an election year, but aside from all that, it was looking pretty good for America. By the latter part of the month things were still mostly normal. I had a great month of photo safaris and actively shot in Wyoming and parts of Montana.

Color

Sometimes It Is Like This

January

Cold Morning In Bondurant

LaBarge Beauty

Standing Watch

Life Is Good

Sunset Glow

Hoback River and Gros Ventre Peaks

Honk When Passing

Foggy View South

Temple Peak Dominates

Layers

Awesome Cloud

Merry Go Round

Stretching, Stretching

Gooseberry Badlands

Orange Streak

Snowy Sawtooth

Untracked Fenceline

FEBRUARY

Something is Up

By the beginning of February it was apparent the COVID pandemic was coming to America. By the latter part of the month, it was uncertain where our future was headed. February was a snowy month with our mountains recording many feet of the white stuff. The photography was excellent. We also made a short trip to Florida, just before the COVID virus began to take hold.

The Canyon

Snowy

Light Pillars

Venus and The Moon

Head Of The Canyon

Wind River Canyon Beauty

Triple Peak Light

Triple Peak and Barn

Well Frocked

Mom and Calf

Before The Sun

A Great Lightup

The Tractor

Amazing Morning Sky

Good Morning

Failing Homestead

Atlantis

Miserable Morning

MARCH

Spring Break and Buckle Up

March is generally the month we enjoy spring break. This year we spent the beginning of the month with dear friends on the western slope of Colorado. I enjoyed seeing some country I had never seen before and the grandness of the Colorado 14'ers.

WYOMING MOUNTAIN PHOTOGRAPHY

Mountain Shadows

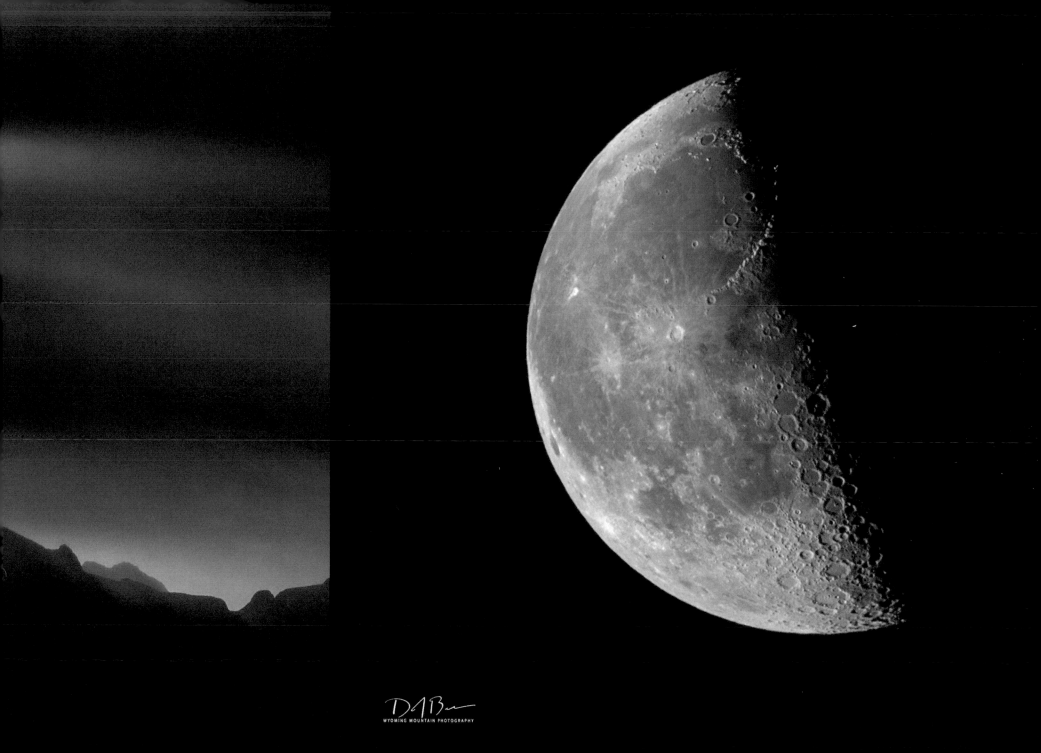

Say Good Morning To The Moon

Morning Fog

Up and Away

Horses-Sleigh-Beaver Slide

Guiding the Team

Sky Pilot Sunset

Helens Light

White Buffalo

This Made A Racket

Sandhill Beauty

Scenery On Dallas Divide

Lights Of Montrose

Solar Flare

Cirque Silhouette

Winter Remains

Sing Me A Song

APRIL

Quarantines

The quarantines began across the country in April. We recorded literally six weeks where things were mostly at a standstill across this great land of ours. This was uncharted territory for the USA, and the world, in a modern, instant communication world of 24-hour news and social media. But, I enjoyed some incredible photo safaris with my wife out in our rural countryside with the Wyoming landscapes and wildlife.

Clearing

Red Tail

Launch

Feed Trough

Busted Dreams

River Rock

Finishing Breakfast

Irritated

Lazy Stream

Sunrise Glow

New Fork Pelican

Moonlit Scene

Springtime

Ripping

WYOMING MOUNTAIN PHOTOGRAPHY

Mom And Yearling

Together

Chilly But Beautiful

MAY

Spring Hope

May usually brings great hope after long Wyoming winters. This May brought more uncertainty but the spirit of the American people was beginning to show. Even though groups were rioting and terrorizing cities in the USA, most of the populace, particularly in Wyoming, were optimistic for better times ahead with approaching summer. With my friends, Tim and Peggy, I was able to enjoy opening weekend in Yellowstone. It was spectacular. I was given an opportunity to photograph an eagle hunting rabbits (legally kept) with a skilled "falconer".

Beautiful Eyes

Gnarly Bitch

Full Moon and Belt of Venus

Crystal

Spring Aspen Grove

North Fork End Of The Day

Into The River

Bears Swim Quite Well

A Reflection From Above

Calmness

Spring Grass

Rebirth

Stem Christie

Beautiful North Cottonwood Creek

Bare Creek Culverts

Beautiful Scenery

Obeying the Rules

Catch the Lift

The Lower Falls

Yonder Lies Jackson Hole

Beauty

JUNE

The Beauty Of Spring

Our spring arrives late at 7,400 feet. It is just the way it is. But, by the first of June, our leaves have burst forth and the flowers are blooming. It is the warmer weather and long days which drive optimism and hope. We had some incredible photography in June; terrific sunsets and sunrises, and green, green landscapes.

Gorgeous

Infinite Beauty

Is This Paradise

Wave Movement

Incredible Sunrise

Rain Curtain

McDougall Reflections

Reflecting Pond

Saturday Sunrise

Spectacular Alpenglow

Such Beauty

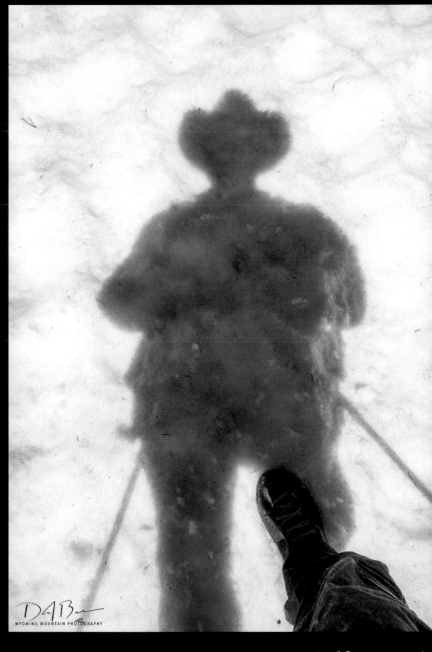

Gorgeous Scene at String Lake

Self Portrait

JULY

Beautiful Summer Month
and Epic Rendezvous Event

July is our month of wonderful summer. The landscape is still beautifully green, the hay fields are growing and the mountains are still mostly or partially snow-capped. But, the highlight of the month was an epic photo shoot of the re-enactment of the original Mountain Man Rendezvous along the Green River, with men dressed in 100 percent accurate period garb. I have included a large section in the book on this event.

Comet Neowise

Comet Neowise

Pinedale Night Sky

The Many Colors Of Early Summer

Beautiful Grouse

George

Fireworks

Primal Forest

Sunlit Grasses

Doc at Sunset at Teepee

Fire, Lies and Eyes

Tugging Hard

Finishing Dinner

Bob

James

Richard

Trapper

Doc

Moki

Hawk

Morning at Camp

AUGUST

Return To Brewster

In August, for the past 38 years I have mounted an expedition of some sort or other into the mountains of the west. I have seen high places and alpine lakes in Idaho, Montana, Wyoming, Utah, Colorado, South Dakota and New Mexico. This year, I was able to return to a Wyoming lake – Brewster Lake in the Gros Ventre Mountains – a lake I once visited fifteen years ago. This incredible turquoise colored gem was just as I remembered it–spectacular.

Brewster Lake and Triangle Peak

Explorers Gentian

Sun on Head of Fremont Lake

Brewster Lake, Triangle Peak (center) and Doubletop Mountain (right)

Morning Sun

Paintbrush Beauty

Going Like The Clappers

Wyoming Night Skies

SEPTEMBER

Smoke and The Blowdown

September will be remembered as the month of heavy dense smoke from western wildfires, which created some remarkably colorful sunsets. However it will also be remembered for an incredible meteorological event which occurred on the western slope of the Wind River Mountains. A strong downsloping wind developed on Labor Day from a deep early season low-pressure system on the eastern side of the mountains. This storm provided a foot of early snow on Lander; but more importantly, generated hurricane force winds which devastated thousands and thousands of acres of forest on the west side of the range. No trees were spared—dead or alive. The forest and trails were obliterated and will remain a major problem for years and years to come deep within the Bridger Wilderness.

Reopening Trail

Tangled Mess

Morning Gold

Golden Dollars

From Mt Airy to Grand Teton

Wind River Range Light

Beautiful Aspens and Foliage

Split Rock

Golden Color

Old Fence Rails

Wonderful Morning Color

Milky Way And Fremont

OCTOBER

Yellowstone and Grand Teton

An interesting phenomenon of the COVID pandemic was record numbers of tourists traveling throughout the American west. Yellowstone and Grand Teton National Parks greatly outdistanced previous record visitor numbers and October, normally a quiet month, was packed. But, I did make two late season trips to the parks including a trip on closing weekend in Yellowstone. Incredible photography, but little solitude.

Halloween Moon Rise

The Geese Know

Momma

Drippy

October

Ranch Road

Great Gray

Fountain Geyser - Lower Geyser Basin

Where Else - Swan Lake

Orange at the Wheat Field

Horses Working Hard

Fall Beauty In The Tetons

Remnants Of Summer

Pride

Eyes On Me

Ranch Gate Shadows

South Cottonwood Valley

Deck The Halls

Fresh Ice On String Lake

Frosty Morning

Mr. Beautiful

Madison River Sunset

Sun On the Ridgelines

NOVEMBER

Move To The Lake

In November we made a move from our house to our cabin on Fremont Lake to avoid remodeling which was on-going at the house. We were able to witness the lake transition from summer "warmer" water, to nearly freezing, to frozen, producing ice as clear as glass, which occurred after the first of the year (not in this book). Watching this 600-foot-deep high mountain lake transition to winter was absolutely amazing.

Squared Up On Indian Pass

Morning Beauty

Icy Reflections

Morning Moose

Morning Granite – Sylvan Lake

Chilly Early Light

Amazing Water And Color

Full Moon Set

DECEMBER

Family and Freeze-Up

The month of December is traditionally a month of family, Christmas and the joys of the season. This year was no exception. We counted our blessings, living in western Wyoming, far, far away from the trials of the big cities and the maddening crowds. In our lives, the year had been a trying one, but not like it has been in many other places. It has been a year of family and the joys of living in Wyoming.

New Fork S-Curve

On The Ice Again

Starry Night On The Green

Saturn Jupiter Conjunction Junction

Beautiful Butte

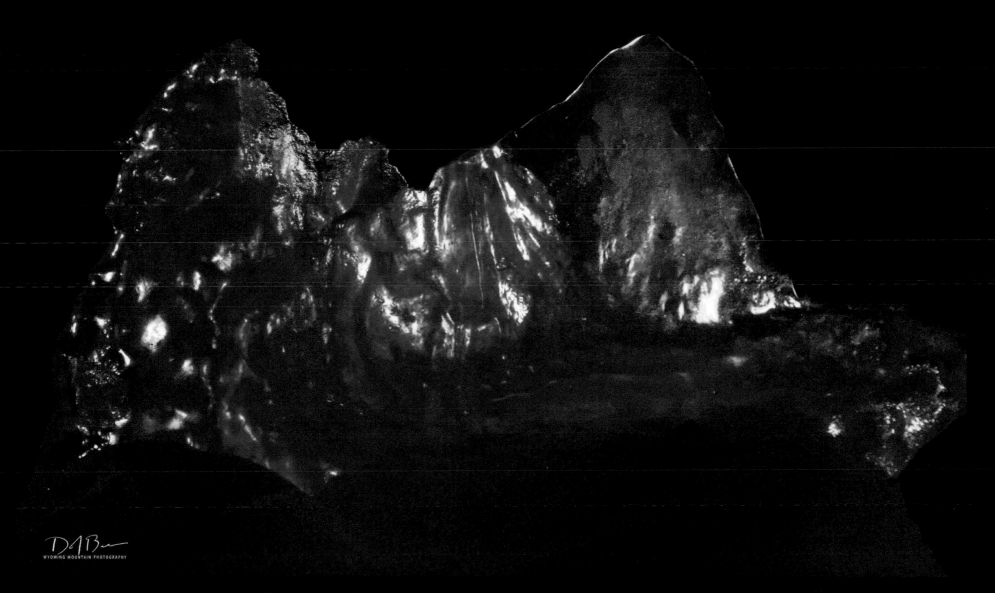

Christmas Ice

Stormy

Frosty Eagle In A Frosty Tree

Cold And Steamy

Don't Try This At Home

Moon Rise

Just a Sliver